ANIMALS IN DANGER

Think of a world without animals. No parrots fly in the sky; no dolphins swim in the sea; no tigers walk quietly through the trees. Nobody wants a world like this, because a world without animals is not an interesting, exciting, or beautiful place.

But the biggest danger to animals is people. Thousands of species of animal are in danger, because people are making a dirty and dangerous world. Are our children going to see tigers, and dolphins, and parrots – or only photos and films of these animals?

The world is changing fast, but there is still time. Read about the animals in danger, and the good people who protect them. And find the answers to the question: what can we do to help?

T0055063

OXFORD BOOKWORMS LIBRARY

Factfiles

Animals in Danger

Stage 1 (400 headwords)

Factfiles Series Editor: Christine Lindop

ANDY HOPKINS AND JOC POTTER

Animals in Danger

OXFORD UNIVERSITY PRESS

OXFORD
UNIVERSITY PRESS

Great Clarendon Street, Oxford OX2 6DP

Oxford University Press is a department of the University of Oxford.
It furthers the University's objective of excellence in research, scholarship,
and education by publishing worldwide in

Oxford New York

Auckland Cape Town Dar es Salaam Hong Kong Karachi
Kuala Lumpur Madrid Melbourne Mexico City Nairobi
New Delhi Shanghai Taipei Toronto

With offices in

Argentina Austria Brazil Chile Czech Republic France Greece
Guatemala Hungary Italy Japan Poland Portugal Singapore
South Korea Switzerland Thailand Turkey Ukraine Vietnam

OXFORD and OXFORD ENGLISH are registered trade marks of
Oxford University Press in the UK and in certain other countries

ISBN: 978 0 19 423379 8

A complete recording of *Animals in Danger* is available on audio CD.
PACK ISBN 978 0 19 423576 1

Printed in China

Word count (main text): 5140

For more information on the Oxford Bookworms Library,
visit www.oup.com/elt/gradedreaders

The publishers would like to thank the following for their kind permission to reproduce images:

Alamy pp 6 (Juniors Bildarchiv), 12 (blickwinkel), 19 (Martin Ruegner/ImageState); Ardea pp
viii (Tom & Pat Leeson), 9 (Thomas Dressler), 16 (Nick Gordon), 40 (Tom & Pat Leeson); Corbis
pp 3 (Bettmann), 4 (Peter Harholdt), 7 (Euan Denholm), 10 (Bettmann), 15 (Christie's Images),
17 (Andrew K/epa), 18 (Amit Bhargava), 24 (O. Alamany & E. Vicens), 26 (Colin Garratt), 37 (Hans
Reinhard/zefa), 38 (Bettmann); Empics p 23 (Doug Alft/AP); Getty Images pp 32 (Karen Moskowitz),
36 (Stan Osolinski); Nature Picture Library pp 13 (Luiz Claudio Marigo), 20 (Luiz Claudio Marigo), 22
(Phil Savoie), 25 (Fabio Liverani), 35 (Anup Shah); Oxford Scientific Films pp 2 (Pat Canova), 5 (John
Downer), 11 (Kimball Ron), 14 (Konrad Wothe), 21 (Robin Bush); Rex Features pp 29 (Sipa Press),
31 (Tony Kyriacou), 33 (James D. Morgan), 34 (James D. Morgan); Steve Bloom Images p 39 (Pete
Oxford); Still Pictures p 28 (BIOS/Gunther Michel)

This book is printed on paper from certified and well-managed sources.

CONTENTS

A Siberian tiger

1   Why are animals in danger?

In 1900 there were 100,000 tigers in the world. Now, there are about 6,000. In India, there were about 30,000 tigers, and the number is now 2,000. You could find eight different kinds of tiger in different countries then. Now there are only five kinds. We are never going to see the other three again.

The tiger is the biggest animal in the cat family – Siberian tigers are sometimes 320 kilograms. They need trees, water, and other animals for food. They usually move about by day, and they go a very long way when they are hunting.

The tiger is a beautiful animal, but it is at risk of extinction. Why is it disappearing? And why are other species disappearing from our world?

Millions of years ago, there were three hundred or more different species of dinosaur. Then, about 65 million years ago, something happened, and now there are no dinosaurs. At about the same time, 70 per cent of all species in the world became extinct. Most of the species in the sea disappeared before that, 250 million years ago. About five times in the past, scientists think, there were big extinctions. A lot of species became extinct, and some different species appeared for the first time.

Dinosaurs are now extinct

These were big extinctions, but animals are always in danger from changes in the natural world. Sometimes there is little rain for years and thirsty animals die because they cannot find water. Bigger animals kill and eat all the small animals, and then the bigger animals die, because they have no more food. The natural world changes, and animals cannot always change with it.

But today, animal species are disappearing faster. This is the sixth big extinction and now humans are the biggest danger to animals. Think about tigers again. People kill them because they are afraid of them. Some people kill them for their beautiful coats or for medicine. Other people kill them because they like hunting big animals. Or they kill all the smaller animals, and then the tigers cannot find any food. People cut down the trees, too, and take away their habitat. In all these ways, tigers are in danger from humans.

But the problem is not just about tigers. About 1 per cent of the animals in the world disappear every year because humans are killing them. We cannot always protect animals from nature, but we can protect them from us.

2 The effect of humans

Do you remember the dodo? This big, quiet bird lived only in Mauritius, in the Indian Ocean. It did not fly, but it was not in danger from other animals there. So it was not afraid. Then humans came to Mauritius. They brought new animals, like dogs, on their ships, and these animals killed dodos. Then the humans cut down trees and destroyed the birds' homes. And some of them hunted dodos – not for food, but because they liked hunting. By about 1680, the last dodo was dead. This happened a long time ago, but we cannot forget the dodo – and we are never going to see a dodo alive again.

A dodo

Things made from animal skins

Animals became extinct before there were humans. But after the first people arrived in America from Asia, 73 per cent of the big animals in North America and 80 per cent in South America disappeared. In Australia 90 per cent of big animals disappeared after people moved there from Asia. Did people kill them all? Perhaps not – we do not know. But they did die.

Later – about five hundred years ago – Europeans visited many other places for the first time. The European visitors changed these places in many ways and they killed a lot of the animals. And still today some tourists visit other countries because they want to kill animals. Usually, they do not do this because they want to eat the animals or sell their meat, but because they like hunting. But in many countries, people kill animals because they can make a lot of money this way. Rhinoceroses die because people want to buy their horns. Some people want to buy the beautiful coats of bigger animals, like tigers. They put them in their houses or make bags or clothes from them. So hunters kill rhinoceroses, tigers, and other animals, and get rich.

Humans destroy the natural habitats of animals too. They put up new buildings and do not think about animals. They make new roads for their cars, or move rivers and make new towns. They cut down trees and take the land for farms.

Sometimes people take dangerous animals from their natural home to a different country. The animals there are not afraid of the new species, and so they do not try to stay away from danger. Black rats went by ship from Asia to the Galapagos Islands. The birds there were not afraid of rats, so the rats easily killed many different species of

Black rats

A cichlid

bird. Some of those birds only lived in the Galapagos. After the rats came, they disappeared.

You can see the effect of humans at Lake Victoria too. Lake Victoria is between Kenya, Tanzania and Uganda in East Africa, and it is one of the biggest lakes in the world. The lake was home to about three hundred species of little cichlid fish and sometimes new species of cichlid appeared. But in the 1950s, the countries near the lake needed more food. From the River Nile in Egypt they took two kinds of bigger fish – Nile perch and Nile tilapia – and put them into the lake. The perch ate the little cichlids and soon many species were extinct.

Tilapia do not eat other fish, but they ate the food of some cichlid species. That also helped to kill the cichlids.

After this, there was a new problem. Most species of cichlid eat the algae in the lake. But now there are not many cichlids, so there is more algae. Pollution from towns and factories also helps the algae, and today – after fifty years – there is five to ten times more algae. When the algae dies, the water cannot move freely. It becomes very dirty. Now the lake is dying, and soon there are not going to be any animals in it. Humans are making the world a dirtier place, and pollution is another danger to animals.

And 75 million people are born in the world each year. They need homes, water, and food – just like animals. Can animals and humans live in the world together?

Lake Victoria

3   Animals matter

In 1996, we knew of 5,000 animal species in danger of extinction. Today, 7,000 animal species are in danger. Perhaps there are many more – we cannot know. So, many species of animal are at risk. Why does this matter?

The world is a more interesting and beautiful place because there are animals in it. You leave the town and go into the country. What do you see? Trees and flowers, but also animals. You sit in a garden and look up. What do you see? Birds, in the trees and in the sky. You visit other countries, and the animals there are different – perhaps bigger or faster or in more beautiful colours. What do you do? You watch them and take photographs of them. Cats and dogs live happily with people in their homes, but wild animals want to be free. How do they live? What do they eat and drink? Where do they sleep? We are interested in the answers to these questions. We want to know about them.

Animals also help us in many important ways. We drink their milk and eat their meat. We make clothes from their skins and stay warm in winter. When scientists learn about animals, they understand people better too. With the help of animals, alive and dead, scientists can help ill people. Many years ago, people were afraid of smallpox. When somebody had smallpox, 30 per cent of the people near them died. But other people did not get ill, because people did not move much from place to place and from

A family of meerkats

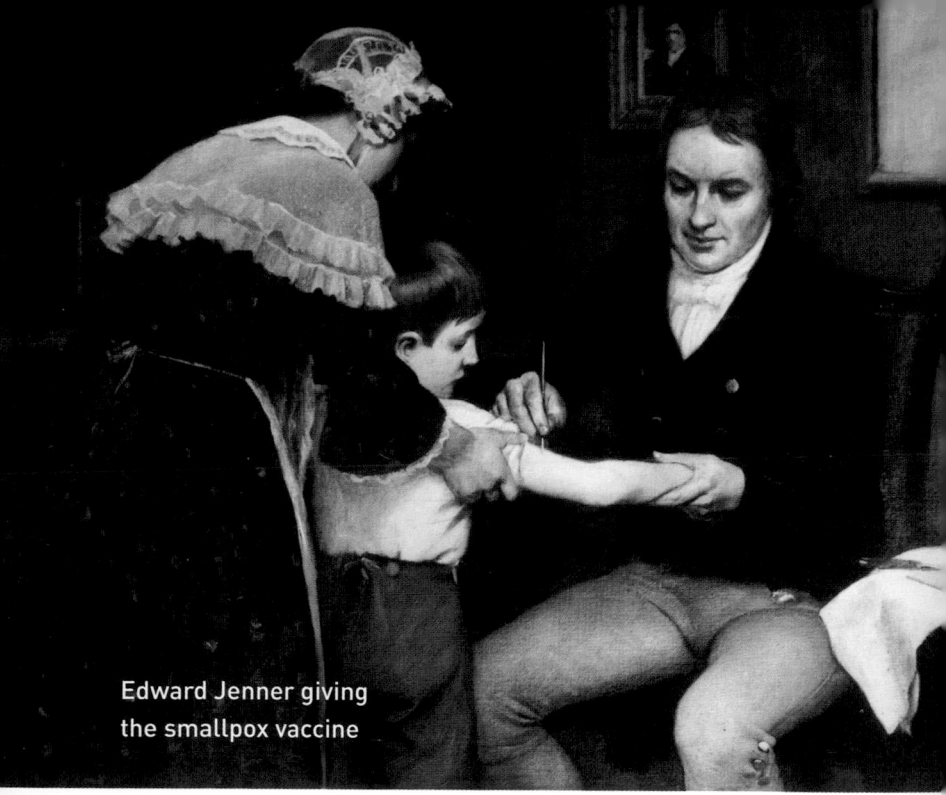

Edward Jenner giving
the smallpox vaccine

country to country. When people began to visit different countries more often, smallpox went more quickly and easily from one person to another. The scientist Edward Jenner found the answer to this problem: it was a vaccine, and it came from cows. With the help of cows, nobody in the world has smallpox now.

Of course, we want to protect animals because we are animals too. Humans do not look very different from some animals. Chimpanzees can walk on two legs and eat with their hands. You can see in their faces when they are happy or angry or afraid. Chimpanzees only live in Africa, and in thirty years their numbers went down from 600,000 to 200,000. People are taking their land. And when humans near them become ill, they get ill too. In bad times we help other people because they matter. But animals matter to us too. Many animals are in danger because humans are destroying their habitats. We cannot close our eyes to this problem. Without our help, a lot more animals are going to die.

We all live in one world – humans and animals. Our land is their land; our trees are their trees; our rivers are their rivers. We want to protect animals because at the same time we are protecting our world.

A chimpanzee

4 On land

To many people, the most interesting animals are the big land animals. We see these big animals on television and in zoos. We take photographs of them, and we are interested in their behaviour. But we do not always understand the dangers to them in their natural habitats.

Tapirs are perhaps not the most beautiful animals in the world. They live on land, near water and trees. They are very quiet. They often move at night, but they cannot go far. Mothers carry their babies for a year before they are born. Then the babies need their mother's milk for a year after that.

Once there were tapirs in Mexico and El Salvador, but no tapirs live there today. There are not many in Panama

A tapir with her baby

The tapirs' habitat is disappearing

now, and tapirs are also disappearing in Chile and a number of Asian countries.

One species, the mountain tapir, has short legs and long brown or black hair. It lives in the Andes mountains, between 2,000 and 4,500 metres, and it is cold up there. But farmers cut down the trees, and the tapirs must move. People hunt them for food or because they like hunting. Other people take the tapirs' feet for medicine. There are only about 2,500 of these animals now, and in twenty years there are not going to be any mountain tapirs.

The rhinoceros, or rhino, is another interesting big animal. Rhinos have one or two horns, and some animals are four metres long. Their eyes are not good, but they can hear very well. They can also run very quickly. In past times there were rhinos in Europe and America, but now all the world's rhinos are in Africa and Asia, and they are disappearing fast.

There are only sixty Javan rhinoceroses. Most of them are in Indonesia, and there are some – perhaps seven to ten – in Vietnam. After a tiger killed a hunter in Indonesia in the 1940s, people stopped hunting rhinos, because they were afraid of the tigers. But now there are no Javan tigers. The Indonesians are protecting the rhinos from new hunters in a national park – but at the same time, a lot of people want rhino horns for medicine. Perhaps our children are going to see Javan rhinos, but perhaps they are not.

One hundred years ago there were a lot of white rhinos

A rhinoceros

in Central Africa, but now hunters kill them for their horns. People buy the horns from the hunters and make beautiful, expensive things from them. A hunter gets twelve dollars, perhaps, but people buy a rhino horn for hundreds or thousands of dollars.

In 1960 there were 2,250 northern white rhinos, in different African countries. In 1980 there were only 1,000. Five years later, there were thirteen. They all lived in one place in the Democratic Republic of Congo (DRC). Other countries wanted to take them to zoos, but rhinos do not have babies easily in zoos. The rhinos stayed in a national park in the DRC and two hundred workers protected them. Hunters could not get near the animals, and the number of rhinos went up to thirty in 2003. Then more hunters arrived. They killed workers, and they killed rhinos. Now there are only twenty northern white rhinos in the national park. Very soon, scientists say, this species is going to be extinct.

Cups made from rhino horn

5 In the water

Some dolphins live in rivers and some live in the sea. The Yangtze (Chang Jiang) River runs across China from west to east. In the 1950s there were 6,000 baiji dolphins in the river. Baiji dolphins can usually hear very well and they 'talk' to other dolphins. In past times they heard small ships on the river and went under them.

But now there are many big ships in the river, and there is a lot of other noise too, so the baijis hit their heads on the big ships. Pollution from towns and factories goes in to the river too, and the baijis cannot see well in the dirty water. When the Chinese built the big Three Gorges Dam across the river, the dolphins' habitat changed again.

A baiji dolphin

The Three Gorges Dam, China

The Chinese stopped the hunting of river dolphins in 1983. They built a home for the animals in the river. It was very expensive, and they needed money for it. People could buy the baiji name, so in China there were Baiji drinks, Baiji shoes, and a Baiji Hotel. Some of the money from these helped the dolphins. But by 1990 there were only two hundred dolphins in 2,000 kilometres of river. In 2004, scientists could find only two of them.

River dolphins in the Ganges River (in India and Bangladesh) are also in danger. About 10 per cent of the people in the world live near the river, so there is a lot of pollution. The dolphins cannot move up and down the river because there are more and more dams across it. There are about 4,000 dolphins now, but these river dolphins are at risk too.

Pollution in the
Ganges River

There are also dolphins in nearly all our seas. They move fast in the water and they play. People in some countries eat the meat of sea dolphins. Hundreds of thousands of these animals die every year when people fish at sea with nets. And when we take all the fish from the sea, we also take the dolphins' food.

Killer whales are from the dolphin family. They live for

fifty to eighty years in the sea, but for only ten years in a zoo. They like cold water, so they can move through different seas. The only danger to them is humans. Pollution goes into the sea and kills the fish, and then there is no food for the whales. Or the whales eat the fish and they are ill.

Whales are in danger from hunting too. In past times the Inuit people of Alaska hunted whales but they did not kill many. Then hunters came from other countries in bigger ships and killed thousands. Antarctica was also a good place for whales. About 250,000 blue whales, the biggest animals in the world, lived there in 1900. Blue whales can live for ninety years. But in one year, 1930–1931, hunters killed 30,000, and today there are only about 5,000 of them.

Other whales are disappearing from Antarctica too. Most countries stopped killing whales a number of years ago, but some countries still hunt and kill whales. And people cannot easily protect animals from men on ships when they are all far away at sea.

A killer whale

6   In the sky

We know of 9,000 different species of birds. Many of them are not in danger any more – because they are extinct. But a thousand species of bird are at risk today.

There are 350 different species of parrot and nearly 100 of those species are disappearing fast. This family of birds is in more danger than any other family. Their habitats – the trees – are disappearing. Many people want to buy one of these beautiful birds and have it in their home. But when hunters take wild parrots from their habitats for this, 20 per cent of the birds die before they arrive in the shops. Today there are no Spix's Macaws in Brazil, because hunters took them all. You can only see this beautiful blue-grey bird in zoos now.

A Spix's Macaw

Kakapos are parrots. They also have the name Old Night Birds because they move at night. They are green and yellow, big and fat. The biggest birds are four kilograms. In a quiet place, kakapos can live for sixty years. They cannot live with people or other animals and they do not have many babies. They also leave their babies for hours at night, without protection. They are different from most birds because they cannot fly.

In 1995 there were only fifty kakapos in the world, all of them in New Zealand. They were in danger from cats and other animals. New Zealand scientists looked for the birds for a long time. When they found them, they took them away to quiet places and protected them there. In these quiet places, kakapos could make new homes and live freely. In 2001, twenty of them had babies. The number of kakapos is going up, but there are only eighty-six in the world today.

The northern bald ibis is not a parrot and it is not very beautiful. It has the face of an old man. It lived in Europe for thousands of years, but now there are no wild bald ibis in Europe. The last bald ibis visited there in 1989. So why did they stop coming? Many birds fly a long way in a year. They leave their homes and stop in warm places for the winter. But often these places change when people cut down the trees or take water from the land. Then the birds cannot go there.

The biggest number of wild bald ibis is in Morocco. The Moroccans are protecting about two hundred of the birds in a national park. In 2002, people saw seven new birds in Syria. But there are also about 1,000 birds in the world's zoos. Scientists want to teach some of these birds to live like wild birds. But birds from zoos do not know about summer homes and winter homes. So some bald ibis are learning to fly behind little planes. They fly behind the planes to a warm place for the winter, and then they fly back to their summer home. In this way they can learn to be free, and perhaps Europe can have wild bald ibis again.

A bald ibis

A zoo bird follows a plane to a summer home

7 What can countries do?

Scientists often meet and talk about animals in danger. Politicians in many countries are beginning to talk about this too. They ask a lot of questions, and sometimes they listen to the scientists.

Who can hunt dolphins and whales? How many can those people kill every year? Can people buy rhinoceros horns? Is it right? Which animals are disappearing fastest? How can we protect them? Where is the money going to come from? These are some of their questions.

So what can countries do? Here is one possible answer: they can open national parks. These are big and usually

Alpine ibex

A visitor in a
national park

very beautiful wild places. Here, animals and birds can live freely, but they are also homes for trees and flowers. Visitors can go there and watch the animals, but usually they leave at night. They cannot hunt or take things away with them.

The first national parks opened a hundred years ago or more. These days you can find national parks in most countries. They are very important because they protect the land and the animals. One of the first was Gran Paradiso National Park in Italy. In 1800 Alpine ibex were in danger, because people hunted them for their wonderful long horns. They nearly disappeared from Europe. But King Victor Emmanuel II of Italy liked hunting the ibex, so his men protected the animals in the national park. Now there are about 30,000 wild ibex, in Italy, Switzerland, France, and Austria. Yosemite and Yellowstone are old and very famous North American national parks. Yellowstone National Park opened in 1872 and has a lot of animals in it.

In 1969, the people of Costa Rica began to protect their land. There are now 160 different places for the protection of animals, birds, and trees – 27 per cent of the country. Thirty-two of these places are national parks. Some of the animals there are now extinct in other Central American countries. These places also help the people of Costa Rica because a lot of tourists come from other countries. The visitors want to walk through the trees. They want to see the animals and birds in their natural habitat. Their money helps hotels, shops – and the workers in the national parks.

Pollution from factories

Politicians can find ways to stop hunting. They can stop the pollution of the rivers, seas, sky, and land too. People in every country are asking, 'How can we stop the pollution from cars, planes, and factories? Let's think about our lives, our work, our homes. Our world needs to be a better place for all living things.' In China in 1990, there were only 1 million cars. In 2004, there were 12 million. But this is only 8 cars for every 1,000 people. In the USA people are richer and there are 940 cars for every 1,000 people. How many cars are going to be on China's roads in 2050 when the people of China are richer?

The number of people in the world is getting bigger all the time. In 1850, there were a billion people in the world. In 1986, there were nearly 5 billion, and the last billion were born between 1971 and 1986. Now there are 6.5 billion people. 1.1 billion live in India and 1.6 billion are in China. Every day, hundreds of thousands more people are born. Can politicians change this? In the towns of China most people can only have one child. In other countries politicians are also calling for change.

8   What can we do?

Can we help? Do we leave the answers to politicians and scientists, or can you or I change things?

Some people help in important ways. Jane Goodall arrived at Lake Tanganyika, in East Africa, when she was twenty-six years old. She wanted to learn about chimpanzees. At first, the chimpanzees ran away when they saw her. But after some time they began to come near her. She gave them names. She watched them and wrote about them. She taught other scientists about them. Then she helped to protect chimpanzees and their habitats – and the habitats of other animals in Africa.

Jane Goodall

Dian Fossey went to Central Africa because she was interested in mountain gorillas. Mountain gorillas are big animals with long arms and long black hair. Scientists did not know about them before 1902. They only live in two places, and there are only about 600 of them in the world. Dian worked with gorillas in Rwanda and after some time she understood them very well. But hunters killed gorillas because they got a lot of money for their heads and hands. When hunters killed one young gorilla called Digit, Dian was very angry. She talked to a lot of people about the animals and money came to her from many countries for their protection. She started the Dian Fossey Gorilla Fund. When you send money to the fund, you get a photo of 'your' gorilla, and the fund uses the money to help the mountain gorillas. Dian was very famous after she wrote her book *Gorillas in the Mist*.

Dian Fossey with a gorilla

The book was then a film, and Sigourney Weaver played Dian. Someone killed Dian Fossey in Africa in 1985. Was it a hunter? Nobody knows. But Dian's work helped the gorillas, and now the number of mountain gorillas is slowly going up.

We cannot all go to Africa, so what can we do? We can stay at home and give money. We can work for the protection of animals from our homes. There are animal charities in every country, and they need help. The World Wildlife Fund (WWF) has offices in forty countries. You can give money or buy from their shops. You can learn about animals near to extinction. Then you can write to politicians and tell other people about it.

You can also make changes to your life. The WWF tells you how. Pollution is killing animals, and a lot of pollution comes from cars, ships, and planes. So can you walk to work or school, or go by bicycle? Or can other people go with you in your car and leave their cars at home? Think about your food too. Do you eat a lot of meat? People cut down trees because they need a lot of land for their cows. Perhaps you can change and eat other food. Then think about other problems in your country. Do hunters kill animals in danger? How can politicians stop them? Perhaps you can write letters or talk to other people about these problems.

Not everyone can make big changes to the world, but small changes by a lot of people help. And your money can protect animals now, before they are extinct.

The Great Gorilla Run — running for charity

9   What can zoos do?

Sometimes an animal or bird cannot live in its natural home. Perhaps its habitat disappeared. Perhaps there is no protection there any more. What happens then?

Sometimes a zoo is the only place for animals in danger. They can live there without danger and scientists can learn about them. Young animals are born in the zoo and one day, perhaps, they can go back to their natural home.

There are, of course, good zoos and bad zoos. The bad zoos are often in towns, and they are old and dirty. The

A hippopotamus in an old zoo

*A young orang-utan
in Jersey Zoo*

A Jamaican boa

behaviour of the animals in these places is not natural. Visitors watch them all day, and the animals can only wait for their food. Many get ill or die.

In a good zoo, people think carefully about the animals. Some animals like living with other animals; some do not. Some animals love seeing visitors and playing, but a lot of animals like to sleep quietly by day. Most animals want to look for and find food; they do not want to take it from somebody's hands. Many animals need a lot of land and trees.

Jersey Zoo helps many animals at risk. There were a lot of Jamaican boas in Jamaica before Europeans arrived four hundred years ago. Europeans were afraid of the boas, so they killed them. Dogs, cats and other animals went with the Europeans, and these animals killed boas too. The boas only live wild in Jamaica, and they were in danger of extinction there. Then in 1976 seven boas went to Jersey Zoo, and now hundreds of little boas are born in the zoo each year. And in Hope Zoo, in Jamaica, people are teaching visitors about the beautiful yellow animals. People in Jamaica are learning not to be afraid of the boas but to protect them.

Golden lion tamarins are small monkeys with beautiful yellow-orange hair. They live in trees in one place in the south-east of Brazil. When people needed this land for food, they cut down 95 per cent of the trees. Jersey Zoo took four tamarins from an American zoo and fifty babies were born in Jersey. There, and in other good zoos, many young tamarins learned about living naturally. Now 140 zoos are helping the animals. Scientists took 147 zoo tamarins to Brazil, and the little monkeys learned to live there. They also moved some animals from their natural home to a quieter place, away from farms and humans. Today 1,000 tamarins live freely. Scientists want to see 2,000 in south-east Brazil in the year 2025; then they can stop their work.

A golden lion tamarin

10   'New' animals

We know about a lot of animals, but not about all of them. We often hear about 'new' species.

Perhaps one of the most interesting of these new species is the okapi. People in the Congo (now the Democratic

An okapi

A golden hamster

Republic of Congo) talked about them a long time ago, but other people did not know about them before 1901. Okapis have wonderful red-brown coats, and black and white legs. They have long blue tongues too! Europeans wanted to hunt and kill okapis, but not all of them died. You can now see okapis in many zoos, and thousands live in the east of the Democratic Republic of Congo.

Sometimes species disappear and then, after a long time, somebody sees them again. This is very exciting for animal lovers. Golden hamsters come from Syria, but many years ago they all disappeared. Then, in 1930, a scientist looked for them and found fifteen – a mother hamster and her babies. Some of them died, and some ran away, but some of them had babies. The young hamsters went to zoos in different countries and now there are millions of them. Nobody found golden hamsters in Syria again for forty years, and today there are no wild hamsters there. But children in many different countries have hamsters now in their homes.

Between the 1880s and the 1940s, people cut down a lot of the trees in the south of the USA, and the ivory-billed woodpecker disappeared. It was the biggest and most beautiful woodpecker in the USA and people looked for it for sixty years. But they did not find one. Was it extinct? Then, in 2004, they saw it again, about seven times. Perhaps it was one bird, perhaps two or three different

An ivory-billed woodpecker

An ocelot – another animal in danger

birds, but the ivory-billed woodpecker is alive and well. Or is it? Scientists cannot agree about this, and people are still waiting for a good photograph of the bird.

We humans live in one world with animals. We know a lot about this world, but we do not know everything. We look for new and interesting animals because we can learn from them. We are finding them, but at the same time we are losing many more. We change things in our world quickly, but animals change very slowly. Many of them are going to disappear soon. We must help them because our home is their home too.

GLOSSARY

algae very simple plants that grow in water
become to grow or change and begin to be something
behaviour the way that an animal or person does things
buy to give money for something
charity a group of people who work to help people or animals
    in need
clothes things you wear, e.g. shirts, trousers, dresses
coat the hair or fur that covers an animal
cow a big female farm animal that gives milk
cut down to cut something so that it falls down
destroy when something is destroyed, it is dead and finished (e.g.
    fire destroys a forest)
disappear to go away from a place; to stop existing
extinct not alive in the world any more; extinction (n)
factory a place where people make things, usually with machines
farm a place where people keep animals and grow food
fish (v) to catch fish
food what you eat
habitat the natural place where an animal lives
human a person, not an animal
hunt to chase animals to kill them, for sport or for food
kind a group of things that are the same in some way
lake an area of water with land around it
land the part of the earth that is not the sea; a piece of ground
mountain a very high hill
medicine something to eat or drink that helps you to get better
    when you are ill
natural made by nature, not by people
nature everything in the world that was not made by people
net a kind of large bag with holes in, used for catching fish
politician a person who works in the government
pollute to make the air, rivers etc dirty and dangerous;
    pollution (n)

problem something that is difficult

protect to keep something safe; **protection** (*n*)

risk (at risk) in danger

scientist a person who studies natural things

skin the outside part of the body of a dead animal

smallpox a serious disease which in the past made many people very ill or killed them

species a group of animals that are the same in some way

tongue the soft part in your mouth that moves when you talk

tourist a person who visits a place on holiday

vaccine a liquid that is put in the body to protect it from disease

way how you do something

wild wild animals live in nature, not with people

zoo a place where you can see wild animals in a town or city

Animals in Danger

ACTIVITIES

ACTIVITIES

Before Reading

1 **Match the names to the animals. You can use a dictionary.**

1 ☐ gorilla   2 ☐ rhino   3 ☐ dolphin
4 ☐ tiger   5 ☐ parrot   6 ☐ whale

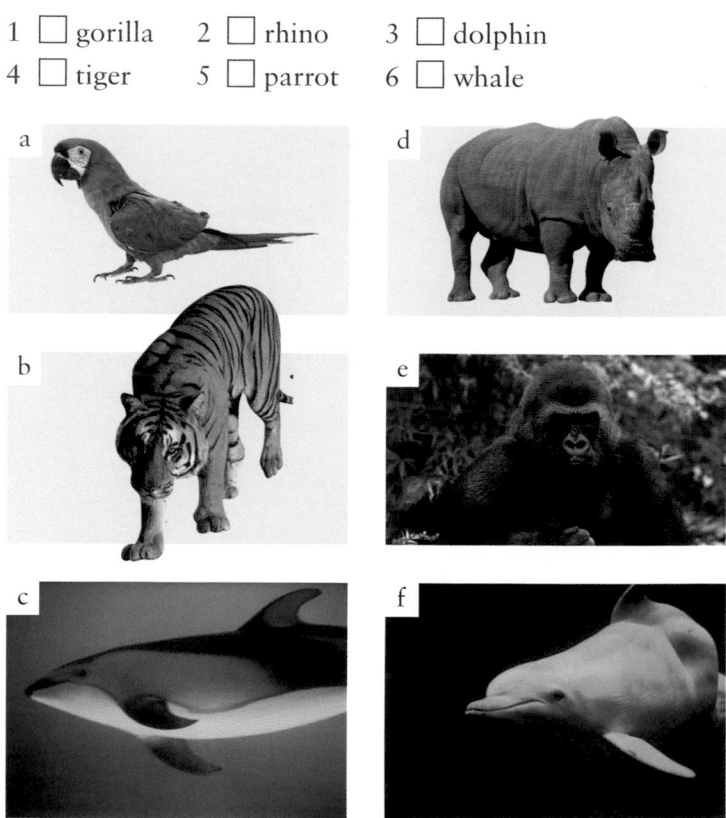

2 **Which of these animals are in danger? What are they in danger from? Are there any animals in danger in your country?**

ACTIVITIES

While Reading

Read Chapters 1 and 2. Are these sentences true (T) or false (F)?

1 Five kinds of tiger disappeared in the last 100 years.
2 When the dinosaurs disappeared, a lot of other species disappeared too.
3 Sometimes animals die because of changes in the natural world.
4 Dogs could kill dodos easily because the birds could not fly.
5 Tourists usually kill animals because they want to eat their meat.
6 Hunters can get a lot of money for the coats of rhinoceroses.
7 Some species of birds disappeared after black rats came to the Galapagos Islands.
8 Perch and tilapia ate the cichlids in Lake Victoria.
9 There was less algae in Lake Victoria in the 1950s.

Read Chapter 3 and then circle the correct word to complete each sentence.

1 More animals are at *risk / home* now than in 1996.
2 We get meat and *milk / water* from animals.
3 Many people want to know about the *life / death* of wild animals.
4 *Cows / cats* helped Jenner to solve the problem of smallpox.
5 When we protect animals, we protect our *jobs / world* too.

Read Chapters 4, 5, and 6, and then answer the questions.

1 Where can you find tapirs today?

2 Why are tapirs disappearing from the Andes mountains?

3 Why are Javan rhinoceroses in danger now?

4 Why are zoos not the answer for northern white rhinos?

5 What problems do Baiji dolphins have in the Yangtze River?

6 What two things are making problems for dolphins in the Ganges River?

7 Which can live longer – a killer whale or a blue whale?

8 Birds from the parrot family are at risk from two things – what are they?

9 Why are cats a danger to kakapos?

10 How are scientists teaching bald ibis about summer homes and winter homes?

Read Chapters 7 and 8, and then choose the correct words to complete the sentences.

cars, charities, chimpanzees, East, factories, gorillas, ibex, king, politicians, pollution, tourists, wild

1 In a national park visitors can see _____ animals and birds.

2 An Italian _____ made a national park because he wanted to protect wild _____ there.

3 Many _____ come to Costa Rica to see its wild animals.

4 _____ from cars and _____ is making problems for many animals.

5 When Chinese people get richer, there are going to be more _____ on China's roads.

6 Jane Goodall learned about _____ and other animals in _____ Africa.

7 There are only a few hundred _____ in the world.

8 Animal _____ work to protect animals in many countries.

9 You can write to _____ about animals in danger in your country.

Read Chapters 9 and 10, then match these halves of sentences.

1 Sometimes an animal born in a zoo . . .

2 In a bad zoo . . .

3 In a good zoo . . .

4 Jamaican boas were in danger of extinction . . .

5 Golden lion tamarins born in zoos . . .

6 Nobody outside the Democratic Republic of Congo . . .

7 Golden hamsters disappeared from Syria . . .

8 Nobody saw an ivory-billed woodpecker for sixty years . . .

a now live in their own habitat in Brazil.

b but people saw one – perhaps – in 2004.

c the animals often get ill or die.

d but a scientist found some in 1930.

e knew about okapis before 1901.

f can go back to its natural habitat later.

g but now there are lots of them in Jersey Zoo.

h the animals can look for and find their food.

ACTIVITIES

After Reading

1 **Match the animals or birds with the sentences. Then make each group of sentences into a paragraph. Use linking words (*and, but, so, because*).**

kakapos, killer whales, okapis, rhinos

1 _____ They live in cold seas.

2 _____ They come from the Democratic Republic of Congo.

3 _____ They are fat green and yellow birds.

4 _____ Nobody outside that country knew about them before 1901.

5 _____ They have one or two horns.

6 _____ They can live for fifty years or more.

7 _____ They cannot see very well.

8 _____ Their legs are black and white.

9 _____ Cats are a danger to them.

10 _____ They are from the dolphin family.

11 _____ They can run very fast.

12 _____ Their tongues are long and blue.

13 _____ When pollution kills the fish, these animals die.

14 _____ They cannot fly.

15 _____ People want their horns for medicine.

16 _____ There are less than a hundred of them in the world today.

2 Find these words in the wordsearch below, and draw lines through them. The words go from left to right, and from right to bottom.

become, behaviour, charity, destroy, extinct, farm, fish, food, habitat, human, hunt, kind, land, mountain, net, okapi, problem, skin, tongue, tourist, vaccine, way, wild, zoo

B	E	H	A	V	I	O	U	R	Y	E
E	L	U	L	A	O	K	I	N	D	W
C	S	M	T	C	H	A	R	I	T	Y
O	O	A	S	C	N	P	F	O	O	D
M	E	N	K	I	F	I	S	H	U	M
E	X	T	I	N	C	T	D	U	R	O
N	Z	A	N	E	T	T	E	N	I	U
T	O	N	G	U	E	W	S	T	S	N
I	O	O	H	A	B	I	T	A	T	T
N	L	A	N	D	A	L	R	L	W	A
P	F	A	R	M	A	D	O	R	A	I
P	R	O	B	L	E	M	Y	K	Y	N

Now write down all the letters that do not have lines through them, beginning with the first line and going across each line to the end. You now have 23 letters, which make the name of a place (three words).

1 What is the place name?
2 Where is this place?
3 Why do people go there?

3 Here is a list of things you can do to help animals in danger. Complete the sentences using words from the list below (one word for each gap).

bicycle, charities, eat, fish, medicine, politicians, pollution, wear, wild, zoos

1 Stop the _____ of rivers and the sea.
2 Do not _____ clothes made from wild animals.
3 Do not buy _____ made from wild animals.
4 Leave some _____ in the sea for dolphins and sharks.
5 Do not buy a _____ parrot to have in your home.
6 Ask _____ to make more national parks.
7 Give money to animal _____.
8 Walk or go by _____, not by car.
9 _____ less meat.
10 Visit good _____ and learn about animals.

4 **Read this report about the danger to animals from humans and circle the correct words.**

Humans can be a danger to *species / animals* in many different ways. Some people like to *kill / watch* big animals – not because they want to eat their *meat / food*, but because they like *hitting / hunting*. In some countries hunters kill *big / fat* animals because they can make a lot of *work / money* this way. They sell the *coats / feet* of tigers or the *hands / horns* of rhinoceroses for thousands of dollars. And sometimes people want to buy animals for *medicine / doctors*.

When people *buy / build* new roads or cities they cut down *trees / flowers* and take the land, so animals often lose their *houses / homes*. Pollution from *cars / bicycles*, planes, and factories means dirty skies and dirty rivers. And there are *hundreds / millions* more people in the world *every / this* year. When more people *leave / arrive*, where can the animals go? Humans make a lot of *problems / questions* for animals. Now we need to change our *behaviour / habitat*.

5 **Choose an animal in danger – from this book, or a different animal. Find some more information about it, and make a poster or give a talk to your class. Look for answers to these questions:**

What is this animal like?

In which countries can you find it?

How many are there in the world today?

Why is this animal in danger?

What can people do to help?

You can find more information about animals in danger from these websites.

WWF: www.wwf.org

Dian Fossey Gorilla Fund International: www.gorillafund.org

Greenpeace: www.greenpeace.org/international

Jane Goodall Institute: www.janegoodall.org

Earth's Endangered Creatures: www.earthsendangered.com

ABOUT THE AUTHORS

Andy Hopkins and Joc Potter worked as teachers of English for many years. Between them, they lived and worked in China, Indonesia, Mexico, Morocco, Saudi Arabia, and Spain. Then they ran English courses in London and in other English cities. Now they live in a small town near Oxford, in the UK. They have written coursebooks, readers, and radio programmes for English language learners, and they have run courses and written materials for teachers. They also edit books for English language learners.

Andy and Joc travel to other countries when they can, and they love visiting national parks. Their favourite trips were to Costa Rica, Kerala (in India), Nepal, and Iguaçu in Brazil. In Costa Rica they saw hundreds of wild animals and beautiful birds in parks in the mountains and by the sea. They did not see many animals in India; the animals were there, in the national parks in the mountains of Kerala, but tigers do not want to meet tourists! At home, Andy and Joc can open the windows in the summer and hear the birds all day while they work.

OXFORD BOOKWORMS LIBRARY

Classics • Crime & Mystery • Factfiles • Fantasy & Horror
Human Interest • Playscripts • Thriller & Adventure
True Stories • World Stories

The OXFORD BOOKWORMS LIBRARY provides enjoyable reading in English, with a wide range of classic and modern fiction, non-fiction, and plays. It includes original and adapted texts in seven carefully graded language stages, which take learners from beginner to advanced level. An overview is given on the next pages.

All Stage 1 titles are available as audio recordings, as well as over eighty other titles from Starter to Stage 6. All Starters and many titles at Stages 1 to 4 are specially recommended for younger learners. Every Bookworm is illustrated, and Starters and Factfiles have full-colour illustrations.

The OXFORD BOOKWORMS LIBRARY also offers extensive support. Each book contains an introduction to the story, notes about the author, a glossary, and activities. Additional resources include tests and worksheets, and answers for these and for the activities in the books. There is advice on running a class library, using audio recordings, and the many ways of using Oxford Bookworms in reading programmes. Resource materials are available on the website <www.oup.com/elt/gradedreaders>.

The *Oxford Bookworms Collection* is a series for advanced learners. It consists of volumes of short stories by well-known authors, both classic and modern. Texts are not abridged or adapted in any way, but carefully selected to be accessible to the advanced student.

You can find details and a full list of titles in the *Oxford Bookworms Library Catalogue* and *Oxford English Language Teaching Catalogues*, and on the website <www.oup.com/elt/gradedreaders>.

THE OXFORD BOOKWORMS LIBRARY
GRADING AND SAMPLE EXTRACTS

STARTER • 250 HEADWORDS

present simple – present continuous – imperative –
can/cannot, must – going to (future) – simple gerunds …

Her phone is ringing – but where is it?
Sally gets out of bed and looks in her bag. No phone.
She looks under the bed. No phone. Then she looks behind
the door. There is her phone. Sally picks up her phone and
answers it. *Sally's Phone*

STAGE 1 • 400 HEADWORDS

… past simple – coordination with *and, but, or* –
subordination with *before, after, when, because, so* …

I knew him in Persia. He was a famous builder and I
worked with him there. For a time I was his friend, but
not for long. When he came to Paris, I came after him –
I wanted to watch him. He was a very clever, very dangerous
man. *The Phantom of the Opera*

STAGE 2 • 700 HEADWORDS

… present perfect – *will* (future) – *(don't) have to, must not, could* –
comparison of adjectives – simple *if* clauses – past continuous –
tag questions – *ask/tell* + infinitive …

While I was writing these words in my diary, I decided
what to do. I must try to escape. I shall try to get down the
wall outside. The window is high above the ground, but
I have to try. I shall take some of the gold with me – if I
escape, perhaps it will be helpful later. *Dracula*

STAGE 3 • 1000 HEADWORDS

... should, may – present perfect continuous – *used to* – past perfect
– infinitive – relative clauses – indirect statements ...

Of course, it was most important that no one should see
Colin, Mary, or Dickon entering the secret garden. So Colin
gave orders to the gardeners that they must all keep away
from that part of the garden in future. *The Secret Garden*

STAGE 4 • 1400 HEADWORDS

... past perfect continuous – passive (simple forms) –
would conditional clauses – indirect questions –
relatives with *where/when* – gerunds after prepositions/phrases ...

I was glad. Now Hyde could not show his face to the world
again. If he did, every honest man in London would be proud
to report him to the police. *Dr Jekyll and Mr Hyde*

STAGE 5 • 1800 HEADWORDS

... future continuous – future perfect –
passive (modals, continuous forms) –
would have conditional clauses – modals + perfect infinitive ...

If he had spoken Estella's name, I would have hit him. I was so
angry with him, and so depressed about my future, that I could
not eat the breakfast. Instead I went straight to the old house.
Great Expectations

STAGE 6 • 2500 HEADWORDS

... passive (infinitives, gerunds) – advanced modal meanings –
clauses of concession, condition

When I stepped up to the piano, I was confident. It was as if I
knew that the prodigy side of me really did exist. And when I
started to play, I was so caught up in how lovely I looked that
I didn't worry how I would sound. *The Joy Luck Club*

BOOKWORMS · FACTFILES · STAGE 1

England

JOHN ESCOTT

Twenty-five million people come to England every year, and some never go out of London. But England too is full of interesting places to visit and things to do. There are big noisy cities with great shops and theatres, and quiet little villages. You can visit old castles and beautiful churches – or go to festivals with music twenty-four hours a day. You can have an English afternoon tea, walk on long white beaches, watch a great game of football, or visit a country house. Yes, England has something for everybody – what has it got for you?

BOOKWORMS · FACTFILES · STAGE 2

Rainforests

ROWENA AKINYEMI

Deep rivers, tall trees, strange animals, beautiful flowers – this is the rainforest. Burning trees, thick smoke, new roads and cities, dead animals, people without homes – this is the rainforest too. To some people the rainforests mean beautiful places that you can visit; to others they mean trees that they can cut down and sell.

Between 1950 and 2000 half of the world's rainforests disappeared. While you read these words, somewhere in the world people are cutting down rainforest trees. What are these wonderful places that we call rainforests – and is it too late to save them?